Angel Up! Study Guide

A Sacred Companion to Angel Up! The Angels' Guide to Ascension

Sue Frederick

Frederick Malowany Publishing

Contents

Angel Up! Study Guide

A Sacred Companion to Angel Up! The Angels' Guide to Ascension

Sue Frederick

Frederick Malowany Publishing

Introduction: A Guided Path to Ascension

Dear Beloved Soul,

Welcome to your sacred companion on the journey of **Angel Up! The Angels' Guide to Ascension**. This study guide is designed to deepen your integration of the teachings, anchor you into your soul's highest wisdom, and empower your transformation through reflection, meditation, and angelic connection.

I'm hoping you'll start a discussion group in your community and use these materials to guide it. We are shifting the consciousness on earth, and all souls are needed to carry the light.

Each chapter of **Angel Up!** carries divine frequencies intended to awaken your remembrance of who you truly are: a soul of radiant light, an angel on Earth.

In this guide, you'll find:

- **Chapter-by-chapter reflection prompts & discussion topics**
- **Meditations and prayers for ascension**
- **Guided journaling and angel writing exercises**
- **Assignments to embody these teachings in daily life**

You may move through this guide on your own or in a study group. You may take your time with each chapter, allowing the energy to integrate. Trust that you are never alone. The angelic realm walks with you, lifts you, and celebrates every step of your evolution. Let this be your sacred workbook of ascension. Let it be the golden thread that binds you to the angelic love all around you—and within you.

With infinite love,
Rev. Sue Frederick
Author of ***Angel Up!***
The Angels' Guide to Ascension

Chapter One

The Soul Lens — Seeing Beyond the Human Story

Summary of the Chapter:

In this chapter, you learn to shift from the ego's fearful lens to the soul's divine perspective. Through personal loss and awakening, you begin to remember that life is a spiritual journey—not a random sequence of suffering. The soul lens reveals that every challenge is pre-designed for your evolution. The angels teach us that the soul sees the divine order in all things. Learning to view your life through the soul's eyes is the first essential step on the path of ascension. Recognizing that Angels are our first responders on earth changes everything for the better. We allow Angels to lift us into our soul's wisdom and provide instant help whenever we're in pain.

Reflection Questions & Group Discussion:

1. When have you viewed a life experience through your human lens only, and how did it feel?

2. What changed when you shifted to your soul's view of that experience?

3. How do you distinguish the ego's voice from the soul's knowing?

4. How does your perspective shift when you look at a challenge through your soul's lens of divine wisdom instead of your ego?

5. What experience in your life makes more sense now from a soul perspective?

6. What does your ego tend to say when things go wrong?

7. How can you begin to practice seeing everyday life through your soul's awareness?

8. What is your understanding of angels and the Angelic Realm?

9. What is your understanding of God or The Source?

Guided Meditation: Seeing Through the Soul's Lens

Sit in stillness with your eyes closed.

Visualize a golden light above your head, representing your eternal connection to a loving God Source.

Breathe deeply and let that golden light enter your body through your Crown Chakra.

Say silently: "Help me see everything through my soul's eyes. Let me view my life through divine awareness. Show me the loving presence of angels even in my darkest moments."

Allow images, emotions, or memories to surface and be reinterpreted with loving wisdom.

Remain in this state for 5–10 minutes. Journal what insights you received.

Angel Writing Prompt:

Ask: "Angels, what situation in my life do I need to view through my soul lens today?" Allow their loving perspective to come through your pen.

Soul Assignment:

1. Choose one situation in your life where you've felt stuck in ego-thinking. Write a paragraph about how that situation looks through the soul lens. Take one inspired action this week based on that new perspective.

2. Choose one life challenge you're facing. Write a journal entry

about it first from your ego's view (fear, blame, frustration), then rewrite it from your soul's view (growth, purpose, awakening).

3. Create a mantra for the week: "I choose the soul lens. I rise above the ego's fear and limitations."

Chapter Two

You Are Never Alone — Meeting the Angels

Summary of the Chapter:

This chapter awakens you to the constant, loving presence of the angels. You are never alone, no matter how dark the path may seem. From childhood visions to miraculous interventions, the angelic realm has always walked beside you. This chapter reminds you to call on them, feel their love, and invite their guidance into your daily life.

Reflection Questions & Group Discussion:

1. Have you ever felt the presence of an angel in your life? Describe the moment.
2. What signs have you received that could have been angelic messages?
3. Share your definition or understanding of God.
4. What keeps you from fully trusting in divine support?
5. What would change in your life if you believed angels were always guiding you?
6. What would change in your life if you believed that God is a perpetual source of unconditional love?
7. What would change in your life if you believed that you are always connected to the God Source; that wherever you go – God is.

Guided Meditation: The Angelic Embrace

Sit quietly, eyes closed, hands over your heart.

Breathe deeply and slowly. Inhale golden light, exhale doubt.

Say silently: "Angels, wrap me in your love. Let me feel your presence."

Visualize a circle of golden angels surrounding you. Feel their unconditional love and kindness. Allow their healing love to lift your energy to a higher frequency of awareness and happiness.

Rest in this embrace for 5–10 minutes.

When ready, open your eyes and write down what you felt, saw, or heard.

Angel Writing Prompt:

Ask: "Beautiful Angels, what message do you have for me right now?" Write what comes. Don't judge or edit. Let it flow from your hand to the page.

Soul Assignment:

1. For the next 7 days, begin each morning by saying: "I am never alone. Angels, guide me today and show me your loving presence in each moment."

2. Keep a journal of signs, synchronicities, or messages you notice.

3. At the end of the week, write a short letter to your angels describing how their presence has made a difference.

Chapter Three

Raising Your Frequency — The Vibration of Love and Gratitude

Summary of the Chapter:

In this chapter, we explore the truth that everything is energy, and our frequency determines our experience of life. Love and gratitude are the highest vibrations we can embody—and they lift us into alignment with divine flow, angelic guidance, and soul truth. When we consciously raise our frequency, we create miracles, attract blessings, and step into our highest path.

Reflection Questions & Group Discussion:

1. How do you experience energy or vibration in your body or environment?

2. When have you felt the difference between high-frequency emotions (like love or joy) and low-frequency ones (like fear or anger)?

3. What daily practices help you stay in a high vibration?

4. What behaviors put you in a low frequency?

5. What stops you from easily shifting to a higher frequency and how can you change that?

6. How would your life improve if you committed to shifting into the frequency of love and gratitude each day?

Guided Meditation: Rising Into Light

Sit in a quiet place, spine tall, hands resting on your heart.

Inhale slowly. Visualize golden light pouring into the crown of your head.

With each breath, see this light filling your body and lifting your vibration.

Silently repeat: "I am a being of divine love – always in alignment with the God Source. I am more powerful than any challenge that comes my way. My light shatters darkness."

Visualize your heart radiating this loving frequency outward into the world.

Remain here for 5–10 minutes. When you're ready, gently open your eyes and journal your experience.

Angel Writing Prompt:

Ask: "Angels, what can I do to raise my frequency today?" Let their message flow through your pen. Trust whatever comes.

Soul Assignment:

1. Begin each day with a 2-minute gratitude prayer: "Thank you for my breath, my body, my life, my awareness."

2. Choose one activity this week where you normally feel stress. Intentionally bring love and gratitude into that moment instead.

3. Write a love letter to yourself from your angel team, praising your vibrational growth and reminding you of your powerful divine light.

Chapter Four

Prayer as Power — Asking to Be Lifted

Summary of the Chapter:

In this chapter, you learn the sacred difference between praying from the ego and praying from the soul. Ego-prayers seek outcomes, control, and personal gain. Soul-prayers ask to be lifted into love, understanding, forgiveness, and purpose. When we pray from the soul, we open to divine frequency and receive the guidance we truly need. The angels respond to our prayers with power and clarity.

Reflection Questions & Group Discussion:

1. How have you prayed in the past—from your ego or your soul?
2. Who are you praying to when you pray?
3. Share some of your favorite prayers.
4. What emotions rise up when you feel your prayers are not answered?
5. Describe a time when you prayed for wisdom or inner peace instead of an outcome?
6. What does it mean to you to surrender to divine flow?

Guided Meditation: Lift Me Higher

Sit in stillness, hands resting open on your lap.

Breathe deeply and visualize golden light descending into your crown and filling your heart.

Silently say: "Dear God Source, Dear Angels, lift me higher. Help me see every moment through the loving wisdom of my soul. Let my prayer be a doorway to sacred understanding and inner peace."

Stay in this golden stillness for 5–10 minutes.

Notice any images, words, or sensations. Journal your experience afterward.

Angel Writing Prompt:

Ask: "Angels, what would you have me pray for right now?" Write what comes with trust and openness. Let them reveal your soul's true longing.

Soul Assignment:

1. Rewrite a recent ego-based prayer in the language of the soul. For example: "Help me get the job" becomes "Lift me into my sacred path. Show me the highest and best way forward."

2. Write an affirmative prayer like this one: "I affirm that I am a powerful being of light who came here on purpose to accomplish a loving soul mission; nothing and no one can stop me." Repeat this affirmative prayer every day and night.

3. Create your personal Soul Prayer. Use this structure: "Dear God Source, Dear Angels, lift me into... (name the quality you seek: love, clarity, trust, purpose)." Repeat this Soul Prayer every morning and night.

Chapter Five

Listening to Light — Receiving Divine Guidance

Summary of the Chapter:

This chapter reveals the many sacred ways angels communicate with us—through dreams, signs, synchronicities, voices, numbers, visuals, and writing. The more we quiet our minds and lift our vibration, the more clearly we receive their divine guidance. We learn to trust the messages that come from light, love, and sacred truth, and we recognize these as uplifting answers to our prayers. We allow and accept angelic help.

Reflection Questions & Group Discussion:

1. How do you most often receive divine guidance—dreams, signs, numbers, intuition?
2. Have you ever dismissed a sign or message that later proved important?
3. How do angels communicate with you?
4. What practices help you tune in to the angelic frequency?
5. What messages are you being shown right now that you might not be fully listening to?

Guided Meditation: Opening to the Voice of Light

Sit in stillness with your spine straight and eyes closed.

Inhale slowly, visualizing golden light filling your body.

Silently say: "Angels, I am listening. Open my ears. Help me receive your loving guidance."

Visualize yourself surrounded by shimmering angelic beings of light.

Sit quietly for 10 minutes. Let images, sounds, or words come naturally.

Journal any insights, signs, or impressions afterward.

Angel Writing Prompt:

Ask: "What do I need to hear from the angels today?" Free write for 10 minutes. Let their light come through your words. Do not edit—just receive.

Soul Assignment:

1. Begin a Daily Angel Journal. Each morning, ask for a message and write what comes.
2. Create a prayer to your favorite Archangel or Guardian Angel.
3. Record any synchronicities, repeated numbers, or dreams that feel significant.
4. At the end of the week, review your entries. Highlight any themes, patterns, or divine nudges that are guiding your path.

Chapter Six

Forgiveness — The Master Key

Summary of the Chapter:

In this powerful chapter, we uncover forgiveness as the most essential act of spiritual growth. It is the gateway to ascension and the vibration that frees us from the bondage of anger, resentment, and blame. Forgiveness is not about excusing hurtful behavior—it is about choosing our soul's freedom. When we release judgment, we rise in frequency and align with sacred understanding. When we forgive, we align with divine light and allow angels to lift us into healing and love.

Reflection Questions & Group Discussion:

1. Who have you struggled to forgive, and how has that affected your life?
2. What's the difference between human justice and soul justice?
3. Do you believe it's your job to judge other people? Why do you believe that?
4. Describe your understanding of Soul Contracts or Soul Agreements.
5. What does a Soul Review mean to you?
6. How do you feel when you imagine forgiving yourself?
7. How does it feel to imagine forgiving the person who has hurt you the most?
8. Why do you think forgiveness is essential to spiritual ascension?

Guided Meditation: The Forgiveness Practice

Sit comfortably, close your eyes, and begin to breathe deeply.

Picture the person you've been unable to forgive.

See them as a soul—not as a human personality, but as a fellow soul on a journey, doing the best they can at their level of awareness.

Channel golden, unconditional love from the God-source into your heart.

Breathe it in. Let it fill your chest.

Send that pure love from your heart chakra to their soul.

Imagine them looking back at you with a smile—full of love, gratitude, understanding.

Hold that vision. Then release.

Say silently: "I forgive. I release. I heal."

Let yourself feel the lightness in your body and heart. Rest here for 5–10 minutes.

Angel Writing Prompt:

Ask: "Angels, what and who would you have me forgive in order to feel inner peace?" Write down what comes. Let their love guide you to clarity and release.

Soul Assignment:

1. Write a Letter of Soul Forgiveness to someone who has hurt you. (You will not send this—it's for your healing.)

2. Then write a Letter of Soul Forgiveness to Yourself. Let your angels help you see yourself through their divine lens.

3. Each night for one week, repeat this Soul Prayer before bed: "I choose love. I choose forgiveness. I choose the soul's view of life."

Chapter Seven

The Seven Stones to Ascension

There are seven stones to ascension on earth. We all experience these seven challenges in our lifetime. We may think of them as obstacles. But they are stepping-stones to sacred awakening; they help us ascend into our highest selves while still on earth.

These are the 7 Stones to Ascension on Earth:

1. **Grief**

2. **Lack of Purpose**

3. **Disappointment in Others (the world-at-large)**

4. **Disappointment in Self (Self Doubt)**

5. **Relationship Struggles**

6. **Health & Body**

7. **Spiritual Crisis**

Stone One — Grief

Summary:

Grief is the most powerful stone we step upon in our ascension journey. It shatters the illusions of the ego and opens our heart to divine truth. Though devastating, grief is also sacred. It breaks us open to the light. When we grieve with love and support from the angelic realm, we begin our soul's healing. Angels come closest when our hearts are broken—they gather around us to help lift our pain into purpose. They comfort us with healing love and empowerment. They teach us that there is no death and show us our beloveds in spirit.

Reflection Questions & Group Discussion:

1. What grief are you carrying in your heart right now?

2. How have your losses shaped your spiritual path?

3. Have you ever felt an angelic presence during times of sorrow?

4. What would your life look like if you fully realized that your departed loved one is still with you – helping you heal?

5. How would you feel if you believed that every heartbreak is part of your sacred life plan designed to help you become who you came here to be?

Guided Meditation: Held in the Light of Grief

Sit quietly with one hand over your heart.

Breathe slowly and feel your heart expand with each breath.

Visualize a golden angel wrapping their healing light around you.

Silently say: "Dear angels, lift this grief. Help me see the divine purpose in my pain. Help me see the spirits of my departed trying to help me heal. Help me see you, dear angels, surrounding me with love."

Feel yourself being held, comforted, and loved.

Stay in this sacred space for 5–10 minutes. Then write down what you experienced.

Angel Writing Prompt:

Ask: "Angels, what do you want me to understand about my grief?" Write without judgment. Let their compassion speak through your pen.

Soul Assignment:

1. Write a letter to the loved one you've lost. Say what's in your heart.

2. Quiet your mind and silently ask your loved one why they left you. Write a channeled loving letter **from** them explaining your soul agreement.

3. Each night this week, repeat this affirmation before sleep: "My grief is my sacred teacher. I am surrounded by love. I

am lifted to see my Soul Agreements clearly, and to see my beloved spirits helping me from beyond the veil."

Stone Two — Lack of Purpose

Summary:

When we feel lost, stuck, or unsure of our path, we are standing on the second sacred stone: lack of purpose. This stone calls us inward, to remember why our soul came here. In those moments of confusion, the angels are whispering, “You are here for a reason. Your soul has a divine mission.” This section reminds you how to reconnect with that truth through intuition, numerology, and angelic guidance. Every detour is part of the path forward.

Reflection Questions & Group Discussion:

1. Have you ever felt like you didn’t know your life’s purpose? What did that feel like?

2. What external voices have influenced your choices more than your inner voice?

3. When have you followed your intuition and felt on purpose?

4. What passions, gifts, or longings keep returning to you?

5. What stops you from stepping up to do your soul’s work as your career?

6. Has numerology, astrology or any other sacred art helped you remember your soul’s mission? How does that feel?

Guided Meditation: Awakening Purpose

Sit quietly and place your hands on your solar plexus (just above your navel).

Breathe deeply and visualize golden light filling your belly and opening your heart.

Silently ask: "Angels, awaken my purpose. Show me the great soul mission I came here to accomplish."

Let images, ideas, or feelings arise.

Say: "Show me my next step forward to accomplish this mission."

Sit in this receptive space for 5–10 minutes, then journal what came through.

Angel Writing Prompt:

Ask: "What is my soul's highest purpose in this lifetime?" Let your angel team respond through your hand. Trust their clarity and love.

Soul Assignment:

1. Write a Purpose Statement in one paragraph: "I believe my soul came here to..."

2. Each morning, ask the angels to guide one small action aligned with your purpose.

3. Reflect on a past challenge. Journal about how it redirected you toward purpose, even if it didn't seem like it at the time.

Stone Three — Disappointment in the World

Summary:

This stone emerges when we feel disillusioned by the world around us—by human behavior, politics, injustice, suffering, and chaos. It's easy to believe the world is broken, but this is a call to awaken to a higher truth. From the soul's view, we came here during these times to be bringers of light, not to despair, but to illuminate. This section teaches us to shift our lens from fear to awareness and remember that light always wins, and love overpowers hatred.

Reflection Questions & Group Discussion:

1. How do you typically react when you feel disappointed by humanity?
2. How would you feel if you knew that the light always wins?
3. What would your life look like if you knew that love is more powerful than hate?
4. What helps you shift your perspective into wisdom, compassion or higher understanding?
5. In what ways can you be a light in a world that feels dark?
6. Ask yourself if your anger at the world helps or hinders you energetically.

Guided Meditation: Lifting the World into Light

Sit in a quiet space with eyes closed.

Inhale deeply and imagine your heart glowing with radiant golden light.

Visualize the Earth in front of you—see its pain, conflict, and sorrow.

Send golden loving light from your heart to the planet, saying: "My light heals this world. I lift the world with love."

Imagine the Earth slowly brightening and healing. See light filling all the dark crevices.

Rest in this vision for 5–10 minutes and journal how it felt to send light instead of fear or anger into the world.

Angel Writing Prompt:

Ask: "Angels, how can I be a source of healing in this troubled world?" Let their guidance show you how to serve from a place of love and strength.

Soul Assignment:

1. Challenge yourself to walk into a stressful situation and only feel gratitude, compassion and unconditional love.

2. Take one loving action this week: help someone in need, lift someone's spirits by telling them how awesome they are, tell a complete stranger how beautiful they are, call a friend who has differing political views and share happy memories with

them.

3. At the end of the week, journal about how these actions shifted your energy and brought you closer to your soul purpose.

Stone Four — Self-Doubt

Summary:

Self-doubt is one of the most persistent obstacles on the ascension path. It arises when we forget who we truly are—a radiant soul with divine gifts who came here on purpose. This stone appears when the ego voice becomes louder than the soul's wisdom. Yet every time we doubt ourselves, the angels whisper: "You are a perfect divine being on an excellent earthly mission to help shift consciousness. You are light taking human form." This section reminds us how to dissolve self-doubt by reconnecting with our soul's truth, remembering our divine purpose, and calling on the angelic realm to lift us above our ego's limited beliefs and stories.

Reflection Questions & Group Discussion:

1. What situations trigger self-doubt in you?
2. How do you feel when you're in that situation?
3. What is your inner critic most likely to say, and how does it affect you?
4. What would your life look like if you knew that you're a perfect divine being taking a temporary human form?
5. What would your life look like if you believed that your

earthly "flaws" are divinely guiding you to accomplish your soul's greatest mission?

6. Do you believe that anyone on earth is a perfect human?
7. How would it feel to remember that all humans are imperfect; and perfection only exists in our souls and in the heavenly realms?

Guided Meditation: Remembering Who You Really Are

Sit in a quiet place and close your eyes.

Visualize yourself standing in front of a radiant angel holding a mirror of light.

In that mirror, you see your true self, your soul—glowing, powerful, beautiful.

Silently say: "Help me remember who I am. Help me see my gorgeous soul and not focus on my imperfect human self."

Let the mirror reflect your soul's gifts. Sit in that light for 5–10 minutes.

Journal what you saw, felt, or remembered.

Angel Writing Prompt:

Ask: "Angels, what do you want me to know about my earthly purpose?" Allow their loving response to fill your heart and dissolve your doubt.

Soul Assignment:

1. Write a short story about your life journey – highlight the moments when you found courage, opened your heart, truly loved someone, or tried and tried again. Review those moments and love your soul for its goodness and courage.

2. Attend a class, read a book or engage in a conversation where you only discuss life through the soul's lens.

3. Each day this week, stand in front of a mirror and speak this aloud: "I am a powerful soul of light. I trust my higher self to guide me."

Stone Five — Relationship Turmoil

Summary:

One of the most sacred—and challenging—stones on the path to ascension is relationship turmoil. These moments are not punishments; they are invitations to grow, heal, and evolve. Every soul we connect with is part of a divine agreement, designed to inspire our awakening. When relationships shift, break, or challenge us, we are being asked to release control, and remember our sacred soul contracts. This section invites you to see relationship pain through the soul lens and let the angels help you rise above the drama and into the wisdom of your higher self.

Reflection Questions & Group Discussion:

1. What relationship in your life has caused the most pain or awakening?

2. What role does your ego play in conflict?

3. How does it feel to reflect on this: The ones who hurt us the most love us the most as souls in our heavenly soul posse. Share your thoughts.

4. How can you bring more soul-centered awareness into your current relationships?

5. Do you believe it's your job to judge others' behavior and why do you believe that?

6. What would your life look like if you believed we each go through a sacred soul review at the end of our lives and then we fully understand the pain we've caused others?

Guided Meditation: Healing the Heart Through Relationships

Sit with one hand over your heart and the other over your solar plexus.

Inhale deeply, drawing golden light into your body.

Visualize the person you're struggling with sitting across from you in a field of light.

Silently say: "I see your soul. I accept that you're doing the best you can to your level of awareness. We agreed to this dance. I release the story that weighs me down in negativity."

Let the image soften. Imagine both of you being wrapped in the unconditional love of the God Source. Feel the angels holding you in light.

Sit in this light for 5–10 minutes, then journal your emotional response.

Angel Writing Prompt:

Ask: "Angels, what is the deeper soul lesson in this relationship?" Write from the heart. Let the angels show you the truth beneath the pain.

Soul Assignment:

1. Choose one relationship that feels unresolved. Write a Letter of Clarity and Release, expressing your understanding of the soul agreement between you for highest good. (You don't need to send it).

2. Each day for 7 days, speak this aloud: "Until we lovingly meet again in the higher realms, I rise above the ego story we've created. I set us both free."

3. Practice one soul-centered action toward a loved one this week. (Deep compassion, speaking from unconditional love, sending golden light to someone you're upset with.)

Stone Six — Health and the Body

Summary:

When our body struggles—through illness, injury, fatigue, pain, or imbalance—we are being invited to realign with our soul's true purpose. This stone is not punishment, but a profound teacher. The body holds the wisdom of the soul and mirrors the state of our inner world. When we fall ill or feel weakened, the angels come close, whispering healing truths. This section reminds us that our bodies are sacred vessels of light, and that the deeper purpose of every health challenge is to awaken and align us fully with our soul path.

Reflection Questions & Group Discussion:

1. What has your body been trying to tell you recently?
2. Have you experienced an illness or injury that brought unexpected spiritual growth?
3. Has it caused you to change something in your life? Why or why not?
4. How do you treat your body—more like a vessel for love or a source of frustration?
5. What would shift if you viewed your body as a divine messenger from your soul?
6. What would shift if you remembered that your body is only

a shell for your soul, and that your spirit can lift above the body at any moment for nourishment and healing?

Guided Meditation: Listening to the Body's Wisdom

Sit in a peaceful space with your hands over your heart and belly.

Inhale deeply, inviting golden light into your entire body.

Ask silently: "Dear body, what do you need me to hear?"

Let the Angels lift you above your body to see your life from a higher perspective. Ask to be shown what needs to be changed, healed or reinvented. Receive what they are telling you.

Rest in stillness for 5–10 minutes and journal what came through.

Angel Writing Prompt:

Ask: "Angels, how can I support healing in my body? What do I need to change in my life?" Allow their guidance to come through you in loving, empowering words.

Soul Assignment:

1. Write a Letter of Gratitude to your body for all it has carried you through. Talk to it from higher self and acknowledge that every health issue is a blessing of redirection.

2. Choose one positive action to begin this week—something nourishing for your body, mind, and soul. (Examples: daily walks, clean eating, joyful movement, breath work, stretching.)

3. Reflect on the changes and tweaks you need to make and create a plan of action.

4. Each night, place your hands over your heart and repeat: "Thank you, body. I love you. I am listening."

Stone Seven — Spiritual Crisis

Summary:

Spiritual crisis is the most transformative of the seven stones. It often arises when we feel devastating grief, disconnected from purpose, or abandoned by divine support. We forget that we are sacred beings greater than any challenge or circumstance. We forget that God is a perpetual source of unconditional love that rules this universe and flows through each of us. Our crisis of faith can manifest as anger, anxiety, depression, or existential fear. Yet this crisis is not an ending—it's a sacred turning point. The angels remind us that even when we feel lost in the dark, we are being called to realign with our higher soul and its loving wisdom. This section invites you to see your spiritual breakdown as the beginning of a spiritual awakening.

Reflection Questions & Group Discussion:

1. Have you ever experienced a dark night of the soul? What triggered it?

2. What beliefs or illusions crumbled during that time?

3. How did it ultimately shift your perspective or spiritual path?

4. Which belief do you align with most and why:

- God controls every event in your life and if you live righteously only good things will happen.
- Your higher soul chose to incarnate on earth for a purpose, and you are always enveloped in God's love and support.

Reflect on how these two beliefs impact your emotions and overall perspective.

Guided Meditation: Rising from the Spiritual Abyss

Sit in a quiet space and close your eyes.

Imagine yourself going through your daily activities and only seeing half of your reality because you have blinders on. These blinders only allow you to see the meaningless details of life.

Above you is an illuminating golden light—it reveals your soul's higher purpose and all of the divine beings helping you. It aligns you with love and inner strength. Look up at this higher invisible reality and allow it to be part of your daily vision. Allow it to enlighten your awareness. Accept it.

Say silently: "Even here, I am not alone. Lift me, angels. Help me feel your loving presence."

Visualize beams of angelic light aligning you with sacred understanding and healing.

Rest in this image of rising for 5–10 minutes, then journal what you experienced.

Angel Writing Prompt:

Ask: "Angels, what do I need to know as I walk through this spiritual challenge?" Let their wisdom remind you of your strength, your mission, and your divine support.

Soul Assignment:

1. Write about a time you went through the darkness and found light on the other side. What helped you the most?

2. Create a sacred space in your home—your Ascension Altar—with symbols of your soul's journey and the divine beings who are helping you.

3. Repeat this affirmation daily: "I am light. I am divinely guided, even in the dark I am surrounded by God's love."

Chapter Eight

Claiming Your Soul's Purpose

Summary of the Chapter:

Your soul came here on a mission. You brought unique gifts, passions, and divine assignments to fulfill in this lifetime. This chapter calls you to remember why you came—to move beyond confusion, fear, or conditioning, and into clarity and truth. Through sacred numerology, intuition, and angelic guidance, you are invited to awaken your life purpose and take steps to live it boldly. Claiming your soul's purpose is a profound act of service and alignment with your higher self.

Reflection Questions & Group Discussion:

1. Where have you been most "on purpose" in your life so far?
2. What fear or belief holds you back from fully claiming your purpose as your career?
3. How would your life look if you lived your soul's purpose to make your living?
4. Have you used numerology, astrology, or other sacred guides to reveal your purpose? What did you learn?
5. Are you experiencing a major life reinvention point now? How does it feel?
6. What are you afraid of changing and why?
7. Have you had previous major life reinvention points and where did they take you?

Guided Meditation: Awakening the Soul's Mission

Sit in a quiet space, eyes closed, hands over your heart.

Breathe deeply, inviting golden light to fill your body.

Visualize a scroll of light being handed to you by your angel team. This scroll contains your soul's purpose.

Silently ask: "Show me why I came. Help me remember my divine purpose."

Open the scroll in your imagination. Let images, words, or feelings arise.

Say: "Show me my first step in making this divine purpose support me financially."

Sit with this vision for 5–10 minutes, then journal what came through.

Angel Writing Prompt:

Ask: "Angels, what is my soul's divine assignment in this lifetime and what is stopping me from fulfilling it?" Let their response flow through your hand with love, detail, and clarity.

Soul Assignment:

1. Use your Sacred Numerology Life Path Number to affirm your purpose. (Refer to your birthday and Sue Frederick's numerology teachings. **Use the free Soul Path Calculator on www.SueFrederick.com.**)

2. Write your Life Purpose Statement in one paragraph: "I came here to..."

3. Take one bold step this week to live that purpose in action. (Launch, share, study, teach, write, speak, heal.)

Chapter Nine

Living as an Angel on Earth

Summary of the Chapter:

This chapter is your activation. You've healed, released, remembered, and now—it's time to embody. To live as an angel on Earth is to bring your light into every moment, to walk with intention, compassion, and higher guidance. It doesn't mean being perfect—it means being willing to view every moment from your soul's perspective. The more you live as an angelic being on earth, the more you lift others into the light. You are not just guided by Angels. You are becoming one. And now is the time.

Reflection Questions & Group Discussion:

1. What does "living as an angel on Earth" mean to you?
2. In what areas of your life do you feel most spiritually aligned?
3. When and where do you resist your soul's calling?
4. How can you become a clearer vessel for angelic love and service?
5. Are you willing to do daily spiritual practices that align you with your higher self? What are those practices?

Guided Meditation: Becoming the Angel You Are

Sit quietly and visualize a golden light descending around you.

Breathe it in until your entire body feels filled with divine light.

Silently repeat: "I am a golden being of light. I use my light to uplift myself and others."

Imagine walking through your day using this light to shift all circumstances to a higher more loving frequency.

Remain in this vision for 5–10 minutes. Journal your insights.

Angel Writing Prompt:

Ask: "Angels, how can I fully live my mission as an angel on Earth?" Write freely and openly. Let your higher self and angel team guide your response.

Soul Assignment:

1. Create a Daily Angel Practice: Morning meditation with angels, intention setting, evening reflection.

2. Write a Soul Vow: "As an angel on Earth, I vow to..." Keep it visible and revisit it daily.

3. Choose one area of your life to infuse with angelic energy this week—relationships, work, health, creativity. Observe how everything begins to shift as you walk in light.

Chapter Ten

Angels in Daily Life — Sacred Routines

Summary of the Chapter:

The most important thing you're here to do on earth is Angel Up! Living a high-frequency life means creating daily practices that align you with your angels and your higher self. Sacred routines are simple, powerful rituals that invite divine presence into the rhythm of your day. From morning meditation to nightly reflection, these rituals become portals to grace, clarity, and angelic guidance. This chapter reminds you that your daily routines are the sacred offerings that keep you lifted and aligned. Your first step is to quiet the mind and open the heart.

Reflection Questions & Group Discussion:

1. What does your current daily routine look like? Is it uplifting or draining?
2. When during the day do you feel most connected to spirit—or most disconnected?
3. What small shift in your routine could create more sacred alignment?
4. When is your mind most active and negative?
5. When is your heart most open?
6. Which sacred practices can you incorporate into your daily routine when your mind is most fear-based?
7. How would your day feel if it began and ended with a practice that quiets your mind and opens your heart?

Guided Meditation: A Day in Angelic Alignment

Sit quietly and close your eyes.

Visualize yourself waking up in the morning filled with awareness of your sacred self and the angelic beings helping you.

See your day filled with grace, compassion, gratitude and physical movement.

At each moment, feel angels surrounding and guiding you.

End the vision with gratitude and a smile.

Journal how this ideal angel-guided day felt—and what you can implement now.

Angel Writing Prompt:

Ask: "Angels, what sacred routines would keep me aligned and connected to your love and wisdom each day?" Let their wisdom flow. Let them design your soul-centered day.

Soul Assignment:

- Design your Daily Sacred Routine using the categories below:
- Morning practice (e.g., meditation, journaling, positive affirmations)
- Midday reset (e.g., breathwork, gratitude, conversations with angels)
- Evening ritual (e.g., reflection, forgiveness, soul prayer for alignment)
- Choose one new sacred habit to begin this week. Commit to it for 7 days and observe how it shifts your energy.
- At the end of each day, journal this sentence: "Today, I walked with angels when I..."

Chapter Eleven

Sharing the Light

Summary of the Chapter

This chapter invites readers to fully embody their angelic nature and serve as light-bearers on Earth. It marks a pivotal shift in consciousness—where the soul leads instead of the ego, and where spiritual service becomes a sacred daily practice. Readers are reminded that this shift into angelic presence while still on earth is a new occurrence, and is necessary for humanity's collective awakening. No soul will be left behind.

Key Takeaways:

- When you realize you are an angelic being on Earth, you ascend to a higher frequency of love, wisdom, and compassion.
- You now serve the world from the divine frequency, while still remaining in human form.
- Earth is evolving. Humans are called to live from the soul, not the ego.
- Long ago you agreed to your life plan - with the guidance of your soul posse and angels.
- Your awakening contributes to a collective global ascension that is actively underway.
- Spiritual practice is essential to stay aligned, and the angels are here to lift and guide you.
- A new vow emerges: to live as an awakened soul and choose love over fear in every moment.

Group Discussion and Reflection Questions

1. Share a time when you felt you were acting from your soul, not your ego.
2. Discuss how fear shows up in your life and how you're learning to override it with angelic guidance.

3. Explore how committing to alignment with your soul's perspective can transform relationships and career paths.
4. What does "walking in the light" mean in your current life circumstances?
5. In what moments do you feel most aligned with soul rather than ego?
6. How have your past struggles prepared you to live as an angelic being on Earth?
7. What fears hold you back from fully stepping into your angelic awareness on earth?

Guided Writing Exercise:

Prompt: "I am ready to serve the world as my angelic self. The light I bring is..." Write freely for 10 minutes. Let your angelic wisdom flow onto the page without editing.

Daily Practice: Soul Service Vow

Repeat this affirmation each morning: "I pledge to spend the rest of my human life as an awakened soul. I will remember that I am an angelic being of light. In every challenge I face, I will carry love and compassion, see the higher purpose, and help others awaken."

Meditation: Activating Your Angelic Frequency

Sit quietly and breathe deeply.

Visualize yourself surrounded by radiant light.

Whisper this prayer: "Beloved angels, lift me, love me, heal me, help me."

Feel your frequency rise as your soul steps forward to lead your day.

Soul Assignment

1. Write a short story describing your future life and how it unfolds gracefully (now that you're aligning with your angelic self instead of the ego).

2. Write your personal Soul Service Vow using the words and ideas that resonate with you.

Chapter Twelve

Ascension Now — The Planetary Shift

Summary of the Chapter:

We are living at the tipping point of consciousness on Earth—where light and dark are at their highest intensity. This is the time of ascension. You are being called to rise, to see beyond the illusion of death and separation, and to remember your divine purpose. The angels are walking beside us, reminding us that love always wins. This chapter teaches us how to live as angelic beings in action, aligned with divine order, compassion, and the light of higher consciousness.

Reflection Questions & Group Discussion:

1. How do you experience the rising contrast of light and dark in your daily life?

2. In what ways have you begun to lift your focus from human problems to divine understanding?

3. What does it mean to you to walk this lifetime as an "awakened angelic soul"?

4. How can you support others who are struggling to awaken?

5. What advice does your Angelic Self offer to help you heal your life?

Guided Meditation: Rising into Ascension

Sit quietly with your eyes closed and one hand over your heart.

Breathe deeply and visualize golden light pouring from above into your crown.

See this light dissolving all fear, confusion, and separation.

Silently say: "I align with my soul's ascension while still on earth. I see only light. I send only love."

See yourself surrounded by angels, guiding you forward.

Remain in this radiant stillness for 5–10 minutes. Then journal what you felt, saw, or heard.

Angel Writing Prompt:

Ask: "Angels, what is my role in this planetary shift?" Write freely, allowing their divine vision for your life to flow through your hand.

Soul Assignment:

1. Write a list of 3 ways you can walk your daily life as an angelic soul (e.g., acts of kindness, forgiveness, intuitive listening).

2. Reach out this week to someone you've been estranged from—with compassion, not conflict.

3. Begin a daily practice of Ascension Alignment: Morning meditation, midday angel conversation, evening gratitude and blessings.

4. Write and speak this affirmation each morning: "I am an angelic being of love and light. I am here on purpose, fully aligned with divine guidance."

Chapter Thirteen

Appendix A: Sacred Numerology

Summary:

Sacred numerology reveals the divine architecture of your soul's journey. By understanding the vibration of your birthdate, you unlock insight into your soul's purpose, soul agreements and destiny path. The Angel Up! appendix interprets your Life Path Number and its meaning. Numerology is a powerful tool for angelic alignment, intuitive clarity, and remembering why you came here. **(Use the free Soul Path Calculator on www.SueFrederick.com)**

The Gifts and Challenges of Life Paths

- Life Path 1: Leader, innovator, courageous pioneer. Challenge: loneliness, stubbornness, fear of vulnerability.
- Life Path 2: Peacemaker, intuitive, supportive guide. Challenge: fear of conflict, people-pleasing, indecision.
- Life Path 3: Creative communicator, artist, joyful soul. Challenge: self-doubt, emotional ups and downs, scattered focus.
- Life Path 4: Builder, organizer, practical foundation-layer. Challenge: rigidity, fear of change, stubborn patterns.
- Life Path 5: Freedom-seeker, adventurer, catalyst for change. Challenge: restlessness, impulsiveness, escapism.
- Life Path 6: Nurturer, healer, compassionate guide for others. Challenge: over-responsibility, self-sacrifice, control issues.
- Life Path 7: Spiritual seeker, wise soul, researcher of truth. Challenge: isolation, cynicism, fear of imperfection.
- Life Path 8: Manifestor of success, powerhouse leader, teacher of abundance. Challenge: workaholism, material obsession, disconnection from the heart.
- Life Path 9: Humanitarian, old soul, teacher of unconditional love. Challenge: grief, loss, boundary issues, arrogance.

- Life Path 11: Spiritual illuminator, master visionary. Challenge: overwhelming sensitivity, fear of stepping into leadership.
- Life Path 22: Master builder of sacred systems for humanity. Challenge: feeling burdened by responsibilities, fear of failure.
- Life Path 33: Master healer and teacher of unconditional love. Challenge: emotional overwhelm, rescuing others, losing the self.

The 9-Year Personal Reinvention Cycles

Every human life moves through 9-year cycles of growth, healing, and transformation. Each year within the cycle has a sacred meaning and offers particular opportunities for learning and rebirth. When you understand where you are in your personal cycle, you can navigate life's shifts with grace and divine timing.• Year 1: New beginnings, planting seeds for your future.• Year 2: Building partnerships, nurturing your dreams.• Year 3: Self-expression, creativity, emotional growth.• Year 4: Hard work, discipline, building foundations.• Year 5: Change, freedom, reinvention.• Year 6: Responsibility, home, family, love.• Year 7: Spiritual growth, inner reflection, healing.• Year 8: Power, abundance, mastering manifestation.• Year 9: Completion, release, surrender, preparing for rebirth.

Soul Agreements and Choosing Our Life Path

Before we incarnate, our soul carefully chooses the Life Path, the birth family, and the major events that will best support our spiritual evolution. These soul agreements are made with the assistance of our spirit guides, soul posse, and the angelic realm. Even the challenges we face — loss, betrayal, struggle — are part of the plan to awaken our highest gifts. Understanding your numerology blueprint allows you to rise above the human view of suffering and see your life through the divine lens of growth, empowerment, and unconditional love.

Summary of Sue Frederick's Sacred Numerology Teachings

- Sacred Numerology reveals the divine blueprint of your soul's purpose and path.
- Your Life Path number describes your soul's greatest gifts and challenges.
- Life Paths 1-9, 11, 22, and 33 each offer unique lessons for spiritual growth.
- Every human moves through repeating 9-year personal reinvention cycles.
- Each year of the 9-year cycle holds distinct opportunities for growth, healing, and transformation.
- Soul agreements are made before birth with spirit guides,

soul posse members, and the angelic realm.

- Your soul chooses your Life Path, family, major challenges, and gifts to fulfill your divine mission.
- Challenges are designed to awaken your highest gifts and lead you toward soul mastery.
- Understanding your numerology blueprint empowers you to view life through a divine lens of love and growth.

Reflection Questions & Group Discussion:

1. What insights did your Soul Path Number reveal to you?
2. How do the qualities of your path number align with your lived experience?
3. Are there gifts or challenges described in your number that you're currently working through?
4. How can you use your Soul Path Number to live more fully on purpose and fulfill your soul's mission?

Guided Meditation: Aligning With My Soul's Number

Sit quietly with your eyes closed.

Inhale deeply and imagine sitting on a gorgeous veranda having a conversation with your spirit guide – the one who helped you design your life plan and choose your path number. Ask them to fill you with perfect clarity of your mission and gifts, challenges and reinvention points. Listen and receive.

Say silently: "I accept my soul's purpose. I gratefully walk the path I chose."

Let this intention fill your heart and align you with clarity and confidence.

Rest here for 5–10 minutes and journal what you experience.

Angel Writing Prompt:

Ask: "Angels, how can I more fully embody the gifts of my Life Path Number?" Let their guidance flow through your writing. Be open to affirmations, insights, and action steps.

Soul Assignment:

1. Calculate your Life Path Number using your full birthdate. (Add all digits together until you reach a single digit or Master Number 11, 22, or 33. **For clarity use the free Soul Path Calculator on www.SueFrederick.com**)

2. Read the description of your number in the Angel Up! appendix and highlight phrases that resonate.

3. Write a Numerology Affirmation for your number: For example: "As a 3, I express joy, creativity, and truth through my inspiring words and light."

4. Begin a Numerology Journal to record how your number shows up in your choices, challenges, and growth.

Chapter Fourteen

Appendix B: Angelic Support Resources

Summary:

This Angel Up! appendix offers you practical tools and spiritual resources to continue deepening your connection with the angelic realm. From meditations and channeled writing to numerology and intuitive prayer, these are the rituals and practices that can support you on your path of ascension. It also reminds you that you are never alone. Your angel team is always near—ready to lift, guide, and walk beside you as you live your sacred mission.

Reflection Questions & Group Discussion:

1. Which spiritual tools have helped you most on your journey so far?
2. What resource or practice in the Angel Up! appendix are you most drawn to right now?
3. When do you feel most connected to your angelic team?
4. How can you build more consistent spiritual support into your daily life?

Guided Meditation: Calling in Angelic Support

Sit quietly in your sacred space.

Inhale deeply and imagine golden beams of light circling around you.

Say silently or aloud: "Angels of Light, I call on you now. Walk with me. Guide my path. Strengthen my clarity and wisdom. Heal my heart."

Visualize a circle of angels forming around you, each offering a gift: strength, clarity, courage, healing.

Receive their gifts with an open heart.

Sit with them in silence for 5–10 minutes, then journal your experience.

Angel Writing Prompt:

Ask: "Angels, which resource or practice would best serve me at this time?" Allow their wisdom to guide your next step forward.

Soul Assignment:

- Choose one spiritual tool or resource from the appendix to deepen this week. (Examples: channeled writing, mantra meditation, numerology journaling.)
- Create a Spiritual Support Plan: Design your weekly rhythm with these three elements:
- -Connection (prayer, angel conversations, sacred readings)
- -Clarity (meditation, intuitive journaling, numerology)
- -Compassion (acts of service, forgiveness and unconditional love)
- Write this affirmation and keep it visible: "I am never alone. Angels walk with me. My path is divinely illuminated."

Chapter Fifteen

About the Author

Rev. Sue Frederick is an ordained Unity Minister, clairaudient, Soul Regression Therapist, and master numerologist. She channels messages and prayers from the angelic realm and receives wisdom from guides to help people heal grief and find purpose. She uses Sacred Numerology and mystical information in her books and teachings.

Rev. Sue is the author of 11 books, including ***Angel Up! The Angels' Guide to Ascension; Through a Divine Lens: Practices to Quiet Your Ego and Align with Your Soul; Bridges to Heaven: True Stories of Loved Ones on the Other Side;*** **and** ***The Sacred Numerology Workbook.***

Her work is informed by three Shared Death Experiences as well as guidance received from the Angelic Realms during out of body visions. She regularly connects to her departed beloveds for guidance and has helped thousands of grievers connect to theirs. She's an honorary Board Member for the non-profit ***Helping Parents Heal***.

Her **Angelic Ministry** is dedicated to helping people connect with their own divine guidance, remember their soul agreements, and step fully into the light of unconditional love.

As a student of numerology since 1980, she brings a deeply enlightened perspective to using numbers as navigational guidance tools for deciphering the soul's journey. She created the **Soul Path Calculator** (offered free on her website) which has helped thousands of people understand their soul's true purpose and how to move forward to fulfill it. For more information please visit: www.SueFrederick.com

Chapter Sixteen

Stay Connected

Your journey of awakening is just beginning. I would be honored to continue walking this sacred path with you.

You can find more resources, online classes, personal coaching sessions, and upcoming events through my website: www.suefrederick.com

I invite you to join my online community —where we support each other's soul growth, celebrate divine awakenings, and continue to Angel Up together. I teach a 7 week online Angelic Ministry class several times a year. I hope you can join us!

You can also find guided meditations, free teachings, and angelic messages on my YouTube channel: @SueFrederick

If this book has touched your heart, I would love to hear from you.

Thank you for walking this Earth as the angel you came here to be.

And so it is.

Printed in Dunstable, United Kingdom

64815925R00050